Who Are You Calling Vermin?

Pam Ayres

Who Are You Calling Vermin?

A country conflict

Pam Ayres

Illustrated by Joel Stewart

EBURY
SPOTLIGHT

1

Ebury Spotlight, an imprint of Ebury Publishing
20 Vauxhall Bridge Road
London SW1V 2SA

Ebury Spotlight is part of the Penguin Random House group of companies
whose addresses can be found at global.penguinrandomhouse.com

First published by Ebury Spotlight in 2022

www.penguin.co.uk

A CIP catalogue record for this book is available from the British Library

ISBN 9781529149999

Printed and bound in Italy by L.E.G.O. S.p.A
Imported into the EEA by Penguin Random House Ireland, Morrison Chambers, 32
Nassau Street, Dublin D02YH68.

Penguin Random House is committed to a sustainable future
for our business, our readers and our planet. This book is
made from Forest Stewardship Council® certified paper.

To everyone who would like to see a balance in the countryside.

INTRODUCTION

I wrote this as a musical, which I hope to see performed on stage, and on which I am delighted to be collaborating with the renowned composer George Fenton.

Where musicals are concerned, the average length of time taken from the initial spark of an idea to the first stage performance is about five years, and as I am not in the first flush of youth, nor famed for my saint-like patience, I would like to show you, in the meantime, the story and lyrics for my show and unfold it to you as I clearly see it in my imagination.

Who Are You Calling Vermin? is a kindly sort of satire about living in the country, something I have done all my life. I'm not sure if it is a blessing or a curse that I seldom see things in black-and-white. I can usually see everybody's point of view and that makes me indecisive, a ditherer. I always feel suitably impressed when someone says with certainty, 'But you are WRONG!' It makes me wish I had the same clarity. But I know that everyone does have their own sincerely held point of view, so here in my book are my characters explaining theirs to you and giving their grievances a good airing. My characters are both human and animal. They include the constantly persecuted Grey Squirrel, who didn't want to be brought here from America to look picturesque on the lawns of English stately homes anyway, and the sniffily-regarded Dung Beetle who performs crucial but thankless work, improving soil structure and scoffing parasites.

Here are the Poor Bloody Fishermen, unable to afford to live in their own communities, who see their former homes selling at eye-watering prices as second homes or buy-to-let properties. Here are the Coarse Fishermen, shocked and revolted at the pollution of our pristine waterways. Meet the Poor Bloody Farmers who get the blame for the tragic decline of our wildlife, whose government support is being withdrawn and who face an uncertain future. Perhaps be cheered by the children of the Forest School as they build a home for frogs and toads, or saddened by the wisecracking Fox as he performs for you his stylish 'Fox Rap'.

These are just a few of the characters in my show and I hope you enjoy meeting them all. Where I have lapsed into caricature, I hope the subjects won't mind too much. I'm not getting at anybody. Well, maybe I am once or twice, but basically, I'm just looking on and letting everyone have their say.

Enjoy the show!

Who Are You Calling Vermin?

CAST OF CHARACTERS AND COSTUMES

CAST   One narrator, plus five or six actors/musicians who variously play the remaining characters.

NARRATOR	Something understated.
VERMIN	Good animal masks with faces visible beneath.
GREY SQUIRREL	Fur coat. Big front teeth.
ROLLY MOLE	Black velvet coat. Pink hands.
FOX	Ginger fur coat with white-tipped tail.
DUNG BEETLE	Grooved brown carapace.
BARN OWL	White coat.

ELDERLY BEWHISKERED TOFF
Tweed plus-fours, a shooting gilet, a gargantuan cap, tasselled socks, general shooting gear and carrying a shotgun.

TOFFS
Tweed-clad as above, carrying shotguns.

THE POOR BLOODY FARMERS
Farm overalls, carrying bunches of udder cups, wrenches and farming paraphernalia.

SEA FISHERMEN
Dungaree-type waders, rescue harness, turquoise nets, fish.

ESTATE AGENT
Cream-coloured trousers, tweed jacket, brogues.

COARSE FISHERMEN
Typical hats with fishhooks, flies, etc., short fisherman's waistcoats, landing nets, vacuum flasks, big umbrellas.

WATER COMPANY EXECUTIVES

Expensive suits.

AN OLD MAN   Dungarees.

AN OLD FISHERMAN

Beaten-up Guernsey jumper,
collie dog.

THE DISAFFECTED MASSES

Cheap, thin, drab clothing.
They are cold.

THE CHILDREN   Hastily donned, unconvincing
kids' clothes, carrying rubber
amphibians.

FRED THE HEDGEROW SLASHER

Farm workers' overalls, carrying
a hedge cutter, with billhook
tucked in belt.

FOREST SCHOOL TEACHER

Tweed jacket.

YOUNG TOFF   As older toffs.

CROWDFUNDERS   Black beanie hats, loudhailer,
placards.

MUSICAL NUMBERS AND POEMS

I'M IN THE WRONG PLACE

GREY SQUIRREL

DIG, DIG, DIG   ROLLY MOLE

FOX RAP   FOX

BOOM!   TOFFS

THE POOR BLOODY FARMERS

THE POOR BLOODY FARMERS

THE ANTI-SHANTY

THE POOR BLOODY FISHERMEN

THE SHITCREEK RIVER

COARSE FISHERMEN

THE SEWAGE SONG

WATER COMPANY EXECUTIVES

THE DUNG BEETLE SONG

DUNG BEETLE

ELDERLY MISS TANNER

AN OLD MAN

NARRATOR *walks on stage carrying a heavy book.*

NARRATOR Good evening. Here is a dictionary definition of VERMIN:

'Mammals and birds injurious to game or crops – for example, foxes, weasels, rats, mice, moles and owls, as well as fleas, bugs, lice, parasitic worms and noxious insects; also used to describe vile persons.'

Turns to new page.

Facts concerning the GREY SQUIRREL:

'The grey squirrel is a significant factor in the decline of the native red squirrel population in the UK. Greys can carry the squirrel pox virus. Although they are relatively unaffected themselves, the facial sores caused by the disease cause considerable suffering and death to the red squirrel – which is already severely threatened and even extinct in many parts of the UK.'[1]

NARRATOR *stops reading, puts down the book and*
addresses the audience.

NARRATOR The grey squirrel is native to North America and was first released into the UK by the Victorians. 'The first verifiable record is from 1876, when Victorian banker Thomas V. Brocklehurst released a pair of greys that he brought back from a business trip to America into Henbury Park, near Macclesfield in Cheshire.' [2]

I don't suppose the grey squirrels *wanted* to come. I expect they would have preferred to stay at home, don't you?

Because we love our own *red* squirrels. Don't we? *Don't we?* Well . . .

'In the New Forest, Hampshire, between 1880 and 1927 some 21,352 red squirrels were shot as forestry pests.' [3]

 So, we didn't *always* love our own, red, squirrels.

But whether we do or not, we *certainly* don't like those pesky grey squirrels . . .

> GREY SQUIRREL *appears in his grey squirrel mask
> and fur coat.*

I'm In The Wrong Place

A heavy rock song, sung by GREY SQUIRREL.

Everybody loves the red, they bless his cotton socks,
Everyone apart from me. I've given him the pox,
No one likes grey squirrels; with contempt they look at me,
But I am not to blame, for I was shipped across the sea.

Refrain
I got the wrong face,
I'm in the wrong place,
I'm just the wrong race, to be loved.

Abducted by Victorians, the rich and stony-hearted,
To pretty-up the park that Capability had started,
Freed beneath the cedars on a foreign British dawn,
To flick our tails and frolic, and to beautify the lawn.

Refrain
So, blame Uncle Sam,
For the way I am,
Never, goddamn, to be loved.

Nothing could contain us, we were happy, and we bred,
No one ever thought that we would overwhelm the red,
Or face the possibility, harder than the granite,
That one day in the future we would wipe them off the planet.

Refrain
I got the wrong fur,
It ain't de rigueur,
I'm just the wrong cur, to be loved.

NARRATOR *to the audience, chattily.*

NARRATOR No, a great many factions in the countryside are *perturbed.* If you look beyond the idyllic photographs on the calendar, those bluebell woods, floriferous meadows and babbling brooks, you soon realize that there is great unrest, both above and *below* the ground. Take Rolly Mole, for example . . .

ROLLY MOLE *appears in mask and black velvet coat and reacts to the following information.*

NARRATOR I daresay you've all got a nice pair of moleskin trousers . . .

Now, each paragraph is read by alternating, chatty, informative actors.

ACTOR 1 Well, moleskin today is made of cotton but the original fabric was precisely that – the skin of moles. Furriers didn't like working with the pelts – they were tiny and fiddly. It took literally hundreds to make a pair of trousers.

ACTOR 2 An interesting thing about mole fur is that it lies flat whichever way you stroke it. This may help the mole to stay comfortable when travelling either backwards *or* forwards in his tunnel. He wouldn't get rubbed up the wrong way!

ACTOR 3 The unfortunate mole has always been considered a pest, so their little skins were constantly available. Over time moleskin garments have fallen in and out of fashion. Their meat, however, was viewed *very* differently. 'Theologian William Buckland (1784–1856), who famously claimed to have eaten his way through the entire animal kingdom, described mole meat as "vile", rivalled only by bluebottle flies.' [4]

ACTOR 4 Contrary to public belief, moles are carnivores. They do not eat plants. Instead, they feed on wireworms, leatherjackets, cutworms, insect grubs and earthworms.

Dig, Dig, Dig

To be sung by ROLLY MOLE.

Rolly, Moley,
Living in a holey,
Shovelling. Dig, dig, dig,
Furry, brawny,
Digging up the lawney,
Heap growing big, big, big.

Feeding, breeding,
Worm and centipede-ing,
Tunnelling the long day through,
Please don't trap me,
Fumigate and scrap me,
For doing what little moles do.

For I don't eat roots,
And I don't eat shoots,
All that stuff isn't true!
Grubs I take,
And a little baby snake,
And underground insects too.

Moles are solitary,
And very, very, very
Fast. We can dig a long way.
Well, nice to have a pause,
But now to use my claws,
For I like to dig a garden up a day.

NARRATOR Foxes are classified as vermin as well, of course. Oh. Sssssh! Here comes one now . . . this is a most unusual sub-species: it is the *rapping* sort of fox . . .

Fox Rap

FOX *strolls on. He is cynical and worldly.*
He talks out of the side of his mouth.

Well, I ain't too clever and I ain't too smart,
And I maybe ain't a critter with a great big heart,
But I know what's fiction and I know what's fact,
And I know that the odds are against me stacked.

Well, I might take a rabbit and I might take a hen,
'Cos a fox gets hungry in his cold old den,
When his ribs stand proud and his sides feel hollow,
If a hen goes walkies, well a fox might follow.

Well, a fox might follow, and a fox might pounce,
With a flourish of his tail, and a swagger and a flounce,
And he might lope away with his face well greased,
And share it with the vixen for a midnight feast.

But the huntsmen come, with the hooves and the horn,
And the hounds all baying on a frost-cold morn,
When the hell breaks loose in the woodland hushed,
And a fox must run till his will is crushed.

A fox must run till he runs no more,
Till the foxhounds rip him on the woodland floor,
And the wheeling huntsmen revel in the thrill,
And the red-faced women, in at the kill.

So, forgive me friends if I ain't too chipper,
Bring on the trail hunt, drag along a kipper,
And if you got a hen, out among the buttercups,
Well, a tip from the worldly: shut the clucker up.

NARRATOR A lot of people dislike our native animals because they interfere with their lawful pursuits. Indeed, they go to great lengths to eradicate them.

An ELDERLY BEWHISKERED TOFF *appears, dressed in tweed plus-fours, a gargantuan cap and general shooting gear. He is bold, entitled and carrying a shotgun.*

BOOM!

At first, he sings alone, in a ludicrously exaggerated posh voice.

> As custodian of these lands,
> And owner of this hyce,
> It is my solemn duty,
> To protect me driven gryce,
> Protect me driven grouse, by God,
> And benefit me health,
> By roasting 'em and toasting 'em,
> Upon the Glorious Twelfth.

As custodian of these lands,
I know, beyond all doubt,
That I am solemn duty-bound,
To wipe all vermin out,
To rid the land of predators,
And little moley rogues,
Crawling in their cavities,
Underneath me brogues.

Beware you feral foxes,
You rat-like squirrels grey,
You stripy-visaged
        badgers,
The magpie and the jay,
Here comes the jolly keeper,
A sporting man and fair,
Here he comes a-hunting,
With his poison and his snare.

Four similarly dressed TOFFS *now appear, tweed-clad, hopping on one leg, carrying shotguns. They aim two spoken 'booms' skywards to the left, and two to the right, then turn and come back the other way. They join in the song, singing in equally ludicrous posh voices.*

Boom, boom, boom, boom, the ghillie and the stag,
Boom, boom, boom, boom, a most impressive bag,
Boom, boom, boom, boom, the buzzard and the hawk,
Boom, boom, boom, boom, lovely day for a walk!

> See the pheasant stately,
> Observe the partridge plump,
> The snipe upon the forest floor,
> The woodcock in the clump,
> What a fine tradition,
> A noble path we tread,
> Load up a pair of Purdeys,
> And shoot the blighters dead.

You rooks and crows and corvids,
Bang! A cracking shot!
Give 'em both me barrels,
Eradicate the lot,
We'll rid the land of vermin,
For vermin is their name,
Everything is vermin,
If it jeopardizes game.

Boom, boom, boom, boom, the weasel and the stoat,
Boom, boom, boom, boom, catch them by the throat,
Boom, boom, boom, boom, nail them on the gates,
And nosey buggers, bunny huggers, stay off our estates!

The TOFFS *break up and walk off.*

NARRATOR Of course, it's all very well if you've got lovely landed estates. But you know, if you're a farmer trying to make a living on a smaller farm, the future doesn't look so rosy. The old ways are changing. The government isn't going to support them in the same way and it's difficult to plan ahead. Farmers see food being shipped in from overseas, from places where the standards are different and poorer. They are being told to go out and dig ponds, plant woods. They don't know what to make of it. They feel let down, and scared of the future . . .

The Poor Bloody Farmers

THE POOR BLOODY FARMERS *appear and sing*
with harsh, bitter voices.

We're the poor bloody farmers and our future is a wreck,
Everywhere we turn, the farmers get it in the neck,
We're 'driving out the wildlife' and we're 'poisoning the land',
We seem to be the enemy, and we don't understand.

Don't produce the Sunday roast, the crackling and the chops,
Nowadays we're told to go and plant a bloody copse,
Forget about the milk and cheese and everything that's good,
The government advises us to plant a bloody wood.

When little farms are desperate and teeter on the edge,
The government suggests we go and lay a bloody hedge,
We're frightened for our future, for whatever lies beyond,
But nowadays we're told to go and dig a bloody pond.

Government has shafted us; they've got us on our knees,
They're filling up the shops with foreign meat from overseas,
Come and fill your trolley up, it's plentiful and cheap!
If you saw how they kept it, it'd haunt your bloody sleep.

God save us from rewilders and the bunny-hugging masses,
God save us from the placard-waving, vegan lads and lasses,
We worked this farm for generations, no one gives a shit,
We'll flog it to some city type and walk away from it.

We'll leave behind the pastures where our families have grown,
The animals we bred that we were proud to call our own,
We'll put it on the market for a massive money pot,
Some billionaire can buy it and rewild the bloody lot.

NARRATOR And it's not just the farmers who are bitter. What about the fishermen?

SEA FISHERMEN *appear, swathed in nets. They are sullen. They sit along the quay, mend their nets and watch.*

A young ESTATE AGENT *bounces on, filled with manufactured enthusiasm. He has said all this a million times before. The* SEA FISHERMEN *mend their nets behind him and watch with resentment and hostility.*

The ESTATE AGENT *is clutching particulars from which he reads.*

ESTATE AGENT 'A truly charming, traditional, stone-built 1850s fisherman's cottage, fifty yards from the harbour and *on the coastal path!*

'With sea, harbour and village views!

'Tastefully refurbished but retaining all its enchanting original features including . . . *a pilchard cellar!*

'A highly successful holiday let, sold as a going concern!

'Just a stone's throw *from Rick Stein's restaurant!*

'Only a short stroll to the beach! Walk the coastal path! Take a refreshing dip! Relax in the hot tub on your mini patio with free firepit! Pass the time of day with the old fishermen as they mend their nets along the ancient quay!'

SEA FISHERMEN *mouth* 'F*ck off!'

ESTATE AGENT 'A once-in-a-lifetime opportunity! A genuine fisherman's cottage, owned by genuine generations of fishermen, and now available to buy at the *unbelievable* knockdown price of . . . £695,000!'

Now, the SEA FISHERMEN *throw down their nets and come forward in a menacing way. The* ESTATE AGENT *runs off. The* SEA FISHERMEN *sing a shanty:*

The Anti-Shanty

We're the poor bloody fishermen, upon the sea we roam,
We're out in all conditions but we can't afford a home,
The little fishing cottages are way beyond our reach,
Nowadays they're buy-to-lets adjacent to the beach,
We can't afford a semi or a house along the shore,
The bloody second-homers will have got to it before,
We're driven from our villages in every single case,
We've got a load of haddock but we can't find a plaice.

SEA FISHERMEN *dangle plaice.*

NARRATOR But, of course, fishermen don't only fish in the sea. They fish in the rivers too. In the pure, crystal-clear rivers that wind caressingly through our landscapes.

The Shitcreek River

To be sung by the COARSE FISHERMEN, *in typical hats,*
carrying landing nets and vacuum flasks.

Now, river life is dying,
And is turning up its feet,
Along the Shitcreek River,
Where vapours ain't so sweet,
Where water ain't so crystal clear,
Where sewage oozes down,
Along the Shitcreek River,
Where the banks are turning brown.

Farewell sparkling brooklet,
The salmon in the pool,
Good morning panty liner,
The condom and the stool,
Funny that a government,
On thrones of power seated,
Pollutes its joyful waterways,
With sewage left untreated.

Refrain

The Shitcreek River, she is finished,
      she is done,
And the poor bloody fish, they are
      floating in the sun,
Bloated on the surface, and as
      fragrant as can be,
Rolling down the river to the poor
      bloody sea.

Rolling, rolling, rolling down the
      river to the poor bloody sea,
Rolling, rolling, rolling down the
      river to the poor bloody sea.

NARRATOR I mean, it's not all bad news, though. Not for everybody. Not if you're a water company executive or a shareholder based overseas, say. You'd be insulated from the problem then, wouldn't you? You'd still be able to *benefit* from the water company's profits, but you wouldn't necessarily have to *worry* too much about things like investment. Or about the infrastructure being old and not up to the job. Updating it, stuff like that. Not when you can just turn on the old tap and send ordure gushing into somebody else's rivers . . .

The Sewage Song

WATER COMPANY EXECUTIVES *appear, pompous, in suits, and sing to the tune of 'Rawhide'.* [5]

Pumpin', pumpin', pumpin',
Keep that sewage dumpin',
Leave the people grumpin',
That's fine!
Surfers in the sewage,
Don't ingest the fluids,
Lots of folk have poo-ed,
In the brine.

We are unaffected,
To foreign lands defected,
Where water is protected,
That's fine!
Assurances will follow,
But promises are hollow,
Let the people wallow,
In slime.

Outflow from the sewer,
Scenic for the viewer,
Swimming holes are fewer,
That's fine!
Sewage overflowing,
Dividends are owing,
Bonuses are growing,
All *mine.*

WATER COMPANY EXECUTIVES *dance.*

Mine, mine, mine, mine, mine,
      mine, mine-mine.

Sewage overflowing,
Dividends are owing,
Bonuses are growing,
All *mine!*

NARRATOR Mind you, some creatures actually like it. Shit. They depend on certain types of it for their very lives. But it has to be the right sort. Consider, for example, the plight of the dung beetle.

The Dung Beetle Song

DUNG BEETLE *appears, wearing a grooved brown carapace.*

In the cowpat you ignore,
A hundred beetles, maybe more,
Do their work unseen, unsung,
Shaping tiny balls of dung.
We haul them down from up above,
To feed the roots of flowers you love,
Our little backs have special creases,
So that we can swim in faeces.

'Why'd you do it?' you might ask,
'So unsavoury a task?
Digging tunnels long and deep,
What advantage can you reap?'
We lay our eggs in balls of dung,
Warm and cosy for our young,
So that they, without acclaim,
All hatch out and do the same.

Humans mostly, it is true,
Feel ambivalent to poo,
They turn away and hold their breath,
But for us, poo is life or death.
In our long survival battle,
We must search for fields of cattle,
Ever hopeful, but expecting,
They'll be dosed with Ivermectin.*

Once the cows are wormed and treated,
All our efforts are defeated,
We can't live in dung exotic,
Tinctured with antibiotic,
Through the fields with cowpats dotted,
Gymnopleurus won't be spotted,
Search you may, but find you must,
No holes in the upper crust.

*a veterinary wormer harmful to dung beetles.

NARRATOR I'm afraid there's a lot of sadness in the countryside, regret for things past. Especially among the old.

AN OLD MAN *appears. He is remembering.*

OLD MAN Oh, them bloody hay meadows. When I was a kid, they used to make the little oblong bales then, not the bloody great round jobs you see now. There's no way you can shift them yourself; they have to get a tractor with a damned great spike on the front. It's all machinery now. But back then, with them little oblong bales, you could stack 'em, build with 'em like bricks. We'd get hold of the strings and heave 'em around, build dens like, and get inside. Oh, the smell of them bales, it was sweet, it was out of this world. I'll never forget it.

The farmer didn't like it. He used to come after us, cursing, waving a bloody great stick, but we was young, we could run like hell, we left the old geezer standing. He had a great gut. Our mother used to say they lived off the fat of the land, them farmers, they didn't want for nothin'.

And before the hay was cut, the grass was high, up to your waist and full of flowers. Grass and flowers. And insects. When I was a kiddie, I didn't like walking through them hay meadows because of the insects; I was afraid I'd get stung.

Grasshoppers and butterflies and all kinds of bees, it was alive with them. And being by the brook you had dragonflies as well. You know, I think about them hay meadows, and all the kids I played with, and our village as it was then, and I could sit down and cry me bloody eyes out. I could. I could bloody weep.

I used to hang about round Tanner's Farm. I expect I got under their feet, but they never slung me out. I loved it there. I just used to sit in the black barn and breathe in the lovely smells. There was two brothers and a sister who ran it. She used to make butter on the kitchen table. You have to put salt on it, knock it about so the water runs out of it. That's how you make butter.

Elderly Miss Tanner

Poem recited by the OLD MAN.

When I was a boy, our house was bordered by a brook,
With Nature all around us, it was everywhere you looked,
The vole upon the riverbank, the minnow's silver streak,
The barn owl in the rafters, with his wild unearthly shriek.
Mushrooms in their multitudes and hazelnuts on high,
We knew where the rainbow trout would still and softly lie,
Hedgerows with their apples, rosehips, blackberries as well,
Which mothers picked with urgency, their winter stores
      to swell,
Food, in great abundance laid before us on the bough,
Easier to get it from the supermarket now.

Elderly Miss Tanner, in your kitchen dark and warm,
You had a wooden butter mould, a brown hare in its form,
When cows were in the meadow or were cooling in the stream,
I watched you in your kitchen skimming off the heavy cream,
Weary of your labour, you were silent, you were stern,
Elderly Miss Tanner with your paddles and your churn.

The frogs upon the marshy land, the lapwings tumbling flight,
Starlings in their millions, the vixen in the night,
A skylark in the morning air, the rising and the fall,
A bat upon the twilight. They are vanished one and all.

I miss you so, I miss you so, the summers aren't the same,
I miss the swifts and swallows in their thousands as they came,
I miss the little martins as they nested in the eaves,
The hibernating hedgehog in his cosy ball of leaves,
But timber was imported with its blight and its disease,
To cut a swathe through elm and ash and all our native trees.

The roads are filled with traffic; fumes are heavy in the air,
The drone is inescapable, I hear it everywhere,
The country of my youth is desecrated, torn apart,
And Nature, which delighted me, now serves to break
        my heart.

NARRATOR And with so many mixed farms falling away, having
their land sold off and the farmhouses turned into smart
homes, it's not just people who feel the loss. A lot of creatures
depended on those old farm buildings for shelter and food.
Take owls for instance. A huge loss for them.

Barn Owl Ballad

A BARN OWL *appears, sadly.*

Old barns are converted,
Which once stood deserted,
Once welcoming, lonely and dark.
He is lost, the white bird,
Who once could be heard,
Haunting and eerie and stark.

Ponds have diminished,
Filled in and finished,
Where tadpoles reliably hatched.
No banks all a-wriggle,
With blob-and-a-squiggle,
And never a frog to be snatched.

And they are lost too,
The vole and the shrew,
No rodents across the floor skitter.
The sheds and the byre,
They are gone to the fire,
No prey on a winter night bitter.

Mothy-white. Pearly.
Serene. Otherworldly,
The soul of the night-time, the black.
The sombre eyes staring,
The hooked beak for tearing,
The barn owl,
       who cannot come back.

NARRATOR It's loss of community that hurts people,
don't you think? If you grow up in a certain place,
you get to know a whole range of people with
different personalities. You know all the houses, and
who lives in each one. You've probably been into
most of them. You talk to people in the street and
know what's going on. All the scandal! You know
who's friendly and who's a bore. Who will help you
out in a crisis, who's a soft touch, who is best given
a wide berth. And what that gives is a strong sense
of belonging, of being part of something varied and
interesting, alive and ever-changing. How terrible,
then, to see all that crumble away, to live isolated in a
land of ghosts . . .

NARRATOR Here's an old fisherman. He was brought up in this village when it was a thriving fishing community filled with activity: the unloading of the fish, shouts, banter and weary men at the end of the day, going up the single street to their homes and families . . .

AN OLD FISHERMAN *appears, leading an old dog. It is night-time in a steep, single-street former fishing village.*

Dark Winter Street

A slow, sad song, sung by the OLD FISHERMAN.

A full moon is lighting the collie and me,
Here on the street leading down to the sea,
The loneliest place in the coldest of light,
One face of the cobblestones painted with white,
Where did they go to, my fisherman kin?
These fishermen's homes with no fishermen in,
Where is the harbour with fishing boats packed?
The quayside with tackle and lobster pots stacked?
Nothing to see now, deserted and neat,
And there isn't a light in the whole bloody street.

A community scattered, and bitterness rife,
This house where my grandfather lived out his life,
His fisherman's cottage, so special to me,
Now a holiday home. Now a dark B&B.
Our solitary footsteps ring out for the throng,
Those ousted by people who do not belong,
The dog has grown cold, now to walk she is loath,
Her legs give her trouble, well, her and me both,
So, we turn and go home and our walk is complete,
And there isn't a light in the whole bloody street.

NARRATOR Well, old people in the countryside are certainly
having a hard time of it. Maybe it's better for the young?
The young in the towns? What do you think?

THE DISAFFECTED MASSES *troop on.*
They are thinly dressed and cold.

The Disaffected Masses

We're the disaffected masses,
From the discontented streets,
We are maladministrated,
And our homes we cannot heat,
The cost of living's rocketing,
The pay's a bloody laugh,
And if you see a copper,
Kindly send a photograph.

We're the disaffected masses,
And our dreams we can't achieve,
By day we fear the scammers,
And by night we fear the thieves,
We had to sell the vehicle,
The kids'll walk to school,
We can't afford insurance,
And we can't afford the fuel.

We're the disaffected masses,
From the disappointed streets,
You can come and watch us worry,
You can take a ringside seat,
We are frightened every morning,
We are panicked every dusk,
And we wish our name was Zuckerberg,
Or Gates, or Elon Musk.

NARRATOR (*Getting desperate*) Oh, SURELY there must be
SOME reason for optimism SOMEWHERE? Surely ONE part
of the population is having a nice time? Feeling some degree
of HOPE?

Ah! Look there! Look at the children in the Forest School
– they're learning about the environment. They're doing
something positive! They're all smiling and happy!

Hello … er … children!

Perhaps THE CHILDREN *don't look much like children;*
they are all recognizably adult but wearing thrown-on,
childish clothes. Or not.

NARRATOR Tell me, what are you going to do today?

CHILD 1 We're going to build a hibernaculum!

NARRATOR A hebirnacku . . . what?

CHILD 1 (*Confidently*) A hibernaculum (pronounced hi-ber-nac-u-lum) is an underground refuge for frogs, toads, etc., made by digging a pit, filling it loosely with bricks, stones and logs, covering it with butyl sheet and earth and planting over it. Drainpipes are placed that lead down into it in several places, and these should be scratched internally so that small feet can grip the shiny surface.

NARRATOR But why? Aren't there plenty of frogs and warty old toads lurking in our gardens?

CHILD 1 Not at all. Common toads have declined across the UK by sixty-eight percent over the past thirty years. And common frogs have drastically declined as well. Their ponds have been filled in to make way for development, and frogs are frequently killed on roads when trying to reach their breeding sites.

CHILD 2 (*Helpfully*) Their ponds. Which have been filled in.

CHILD 1 Diseases have spread as well, which is another reason
we don't see them. And this is a great loss to gardeners
because frogs and toads eat huge numbers of slugs and snails.

CHILD 2 People don't still eat frogs' legs, do they?

CHILD 1 (*Quoting*) 'The French eat an estimated 80 million
frogs a year (that's 160 million frogs' legs).
Though diners in French brasseries may not know it, their
frogs' legs are most likely caught by hunters in the dead of
the night in the murky swamps of tropical Indonesia and
sold at local markets.' [6]

THE CHILDREN *react.*

CHILD 2 And toads are tremendously important in literature! Everybody loves Mr Toad in *The Wind in the Willows* by Kenneth Grahame, so puffed up and full of himself! And don't forget Kermit!

CHILD 1 We *love* frogs and toads. That's why we're going to make them a nice comfy home!

We're Going to Build a Hibernaculum

THE CHILDREN *dance forward, carrying rubber amphibians as they sing.*

We're going to build a hibernaculum,
For all the frogs and toads,
We're going to build a hibernaculum,
For frogs and toad's abodes,
Wait till they see!
Wait till they see!
The beautiful hibernaculum built by you and me,
They'll never be found,
Underneath the ground,
Sleeping in our beautiful hiber-NAC-ulum!

They repeat the song while holding amphibians and capering.

In contrast to the children's sweet song, suddenly the deafening noise of a hedge trimmer is heard, and FRED THE HEDGEROW SLASHER *appears. He is an older man carrying a hedge trimmer and slashing it, sword-like, from side to side. The children scatter in fear, ushered by their* TEACHER, *his arms outstretched.*

The Slashing Song

FRED THE HEDGEROW SLASHER, *still slashing, comes threateningly centre stage and sings.*

I am Fred the hedgerow slasher, I have slashed 'em man
    and boy,
The slashing down of hedges fills my soft old heart with joy,
When I see a hedgerow looking hearty, green and hale,
I drive up in me tractor and I slash it with me flail.

I slash it with me clippers, and I slash it with me shears,
I like to cut the blossom off as soon as it appears,
Keep 'em low, keep 'em low, don't let them grow up high
I'm Fred the hedgerow slasher and I'll do it till I die.

Hand me down my strimmer, hand me down my blade,
I shall not lay my head down till all greenery is flayed,
Little hedgerow animals, I greet them with a snort,
I'm Fred the hedgerow slasher and I like my hedges SHORT.

He slashes off, a scary figure. Now the FOREST SCHOOL
TEACHER *walks forward and recites the contrasting*
HEDGEROW *poem. The* CHILDREN *are visibly consoled*
by this reading.

FOREST SCHOOL TEACHER That's how Fred sees things but
there's a contrasting view. A lot of people see hedgerows as
massively valuable to wildlife. They see our hedgerows as a
natural larder: a provider of food and somewhere safe to hide,
nest and bring up a family.

The Hedgerow

Poem recited by the FOREST SCHOOL TEACHER.

Now the hedgerow casts its shade,
The sparse, the tall, the neatly laid,
With campions and parsley lined,
And honeysuckle intertwined.
Here a butterfly may rest,
And blackbirds build their sturdy nests,
And little creatures, in the green,
Can slip along and not be seen.

Here may livestock sweetly browse,
Here may sickly sheep or cows,
In the hedgerow's rich allure,
Seek a comfort and a cure.

Then blackberries, and rosehips red,
Sloes and damsons, freely shed
Their autumn bounty – spread the news!
To native birds, and voles and shrews
Come now, make a winter store,

Fatten up, and carry more
To bramble, burrow, crevice, lair,
For when the winter boughs are bare.

Regard again, and celebrate,
The hedgerow, with its beauty great,
Which in pollution, ever rife,
Breathes oxygen,
      to give us life.

NARRATOR Well, that's a more comforting view, isn't it? More positive. Thank you to the teacher and children of the Forest School. Children tend to look on the bright side, don't you think? They have a kind of marvellous natural optimism. Sadly, that trait is less commonly found in adults, even in people you'd think would be ecstatically happy. Because, even in the aristocracy, the landed gentry, things can go badly wrong. The next generation isn't necessarily as keen on administering the ancestral estate as the previous one. The eldest son might well have wanted to do something else. The pressure might have got to him.

> *A* YOUNG TOFF *appears, looking crestfallen, alongside the* ELDERLY BEWHISKERED TOFF, *his father. The older man sings, with the other* TOFFS *in the background, a song of regret. It is still the 'BOOM!' song but the BOOMS are no longer hearty, they are softer and sadder. The estate is passing out of their hands. A funny song but with a poignant thread. They cheer up at the end, having realized that their family have plenty of other country estates.*

BOOM!

(A sadder version)

Boom, boom, boom, boom, the
    news is bloody grim,
Here's me noble son and heir, Lord
    Cuthbert, this is him,
He's sniffed away his future, it is
    drawing to a close,
He took the family fortune, and
    shoved it up his nose.

Boom, boom, boom, boom,
    I take some blame of
    course,
Boom, boom, boom, boom,
    his ma and
    I divorced,
The boy had no security, of
    that there is no doubt,
I liked a blonde and I was
    fond of . . . putting
    it about.

There goes the ancestral pile, there
goes the estate,
Seat of the nobility, since 'Enery the
eighth,
We'll have to think of selling up, of
moving somewhere small,
And watch me noble son and heir,
inherit bugger all.

Rewilders, bunny huggers, now the
place is up for sale,
See if *you* can make it look as
healthy and as hale,
I give you twenty years or so, twenty
years or less,
Before the place is ruined, it'll be a
bloody mess.

Boom, boom, boom, this estate will
    be no more,
Boom, boom, boom, thank Christ
    we've got some more!
Boom, boom, boom, boom, we'll
    shoot now at our brothers,
Boom, boom, boom, boom, let's go
    and shoot at Mother's!

NARRATOR But then, what is it they say? 'One man's misfortune
is another man's opportunity.' The estate is being sold off.
All of this lovely land, rivers, woods. Of course, land is
expensive. It costs hundreds of thousands of pounds. Which
you might not have. But wait a minute, have you heard of
crowdfunding? People have raised *millions of pounds* through
crowdfunding. For all sorts of good causes. The crucial thing
is to engage people's emotions. Don't shilly-shally, don't use
big posh words, just explain what you want to do, and why
you want to do it. Tell it to them straight. Be passionate! Make
them want to help! Say it so that people can't *wait* to give
you their money! Get people in the heart! Be a crowdfunder!
Look, here comes one now . . .

A group comes on stage, led by the CROWDFUNDER,
*an impassioned young man in a beanie hat, carrying a
loudhailer and a placard saying, 'Moles Matter'. Behind
him there is a display, like a thermometer, showing the
amount of donations raised. His aim, and that of his
companions, is to buy part of the estate and set it up as a
wildlife reserve. He is the leader of the campaign and he
sings with authority and urgency.*

The Crowdfunder's Song

People, your attention please, no
        jokes or mickey-takers,
We're trying to raise enough to buy
        about a hundred acres,
Could you give a quid or so? Could
        you manage that?
To make the land hospitable, with
        hedge and habitat,
To welcome back the tiny ones,
        the ones without a home,
Insects and invertebrates who
        live beneath a stone,
All our native species, from
        the scary to the cute,
Frogs and toads and dragonflies and
        sticklebacks and newts.

Donations of money raised on the thermometer go up throughout the song.

We're going to plant a forest here, if
only we succeed,
And give our homeless animals the
sanctuary they need,
We have the volunteers, we have the
will, we have the plan,
Support us if you will, I beg you,
help us if you can,
Help the birds and butterflies, the
mice and shrews and voles,
All the tiny creatures (*relevant
creature speaks*) and the
beetles! And the moles!
I know that we can do this, it's no
fairy tale or yarn,
Put fish back in the river and the
owl back in the barn.

*Money thermometer goes through the roof and
explodes spectacularly.*

We're the internet phenomenon, the
wonder of the age!
The public have supported us at
every single stage,
I only asked the crowd if they could
spare a couple of quid,
To help us raise the money and
incredibly – we *did!*

NARRATOR So, that's grand news! Isn't it? They raised the money!

Cheers in the background.

NARRATOR The animals have all got a home!

More cheers.

NARRATOR Mind you . . .

In the background: 'What?'

NARRATOR They'll still go on eating each other.

Groans, sounds of disappointment.

Red in Tooth and Claw

All of the VERMIN *appear and cheerfully sing, singly and together.*

Nature, red in tooth and claw,
One goes down the other one's maw,
Fox and badger, owl and stoat,
We all disappear down the other one's throat.

It's the way of the world and we're not that keen,
So make it quick and make it clean,
No hard feelings either way,
Each of us is the other one's prey.

What's a hungry fox to do?
We all gotta eat, so I'll just eat you,
We're all realistic in this group,
We eat each other in one fell swoop.

But wait! Great news has come our way,
The land's been sold! Or so they say,
Big Brown Hare a one-minute mile did,
Told us all: We've been rewilded!

No gamekeeper on his round,
No spent cartridge on the ground,
We won't finish up in a cast-iron pot,
We'll eat each other but we won't get shot.

We won't get shot and we won't get snared,
We won't get poisoned and we won't get scared,
We won't get forced to run like hell,
We'll eat each other. All is well.

It's the way of the world and we're not that keen,
So make it quick and make it clean,
No hard feelings either way,
Each of us is the other one's prey.

NARRATOR (*Brightly*) And you never know, everything may turn out all right in the end!

The full cast appears. They have access to copious hats, props and masks, which they rapidly don as they sing.

FARMERS Perhaps our lovely government will give us some support.

TOFFS Perhaps the bunny huggers will respect our ancient sport.

VERMIN Perhaps the population will see some good in me.

SEA FISHERMEN

And people who bought buy-to-lets will all jump in the sea.

COARSE FISHERMEN

Maybe the polluters will
purify our streams.

CROWDFUNDERS

Purify our waterways? In
your bloody dreams!
All will be rewilded, all will
be renewed,
The country will look lovely,

FARMERS But we won't have any food.

FISHERMEN

Our stocks will be
sustainable,
The French will be our
friends, (*aside: 'Bonjour,
mon ami!'*)

ALL (*In a great harmonious
blast*) We shall live in
harmony,
Until the bitter end.

(They shout)

BOOM!

Blackout.

PAM AYRES

NOTES

1   The Grey Squirrels: The British Association for Shooting & Conservation.

2   Thomas V. Brocklehurst and New Forest statistics: Wildlife Online.

3   https://www.wildlifeonline.me.uk/animals/article/squirrel-interaction-with-humans-damage-to-forestry

4   https://blog.truthaboutfur.com/moleskin-unique-fur-favoured-by-high-society

5   'Rawhide' was written by Ned Washington (lyrics) and composed by Dimitri Tiomkin. It was originally recorded by Frankie Laine.

6   https://www.thelocal.fr

ACKNOWLEDGEMENTS

*For their support and encouragement, I extend grateful
thanks to Andrew Goodfellow, Michelle Warner,
everyone involved with producing my book at Ebury,
and my husband Dudley Russell.*

*In particular this time, I want to express my affectionate
and profound gratitude to Vivien Green of Sheil Land,
my wonderful literary agent of twenty-seven years. Her
wise, considered advice and her friendship have been
true life-enhancers.*